A Brief Natural History of an American Girl

POEMS

Sarah Freligh

Accents Publishing ◆ Lexington KY ◆ 2012

Copyright © 2012 by Sarah Freligh
All rights reserved

Printed in the United States of America

Accents Publishing
Editor: Katerina Stoykova-Klemer
Designer: Simeon Kondev
Cover Illustration: Odilon Redon, *Five Studies of Female Nudes*

A Brief Natural History of an American Girl is the Editor's Choice award winner for the 2012 Accents Publishing Poetry Chapbook Contest.

Accents Publishing is an independent press for brilliant voices. For a catalog of current and upcoming titles, please visit us on the Web at http://www.accents-publishing.com

ISBN: 978-1-936628-14-8
First Edition
10 9 8 7 6 5 4 3 2 1

For my sisters: Partners in crime

Table of Contents

Postcard from the Lower Peninsula, Circa 1958/1
Woman's Work/2
A Brief Natural History of an Eighth Grade Girl/3
Blissfield, Michigan: July 1969/5
Billy/6
Donut Delite: 1969/7
Sex Education/8
The Birth Mother on the Day After/10
Safe/11
The Birth Mother on Her Daughter's First Birthday/12
Wondrous/13
Easy/14
Old Flame/15
Depending/16
Notes on "Mother Holding Child," Kodacolor Print, Circa 1952/17
Lullaby for the Daughter I Gave Away/19
Waitress/21

Postcard from the Lower Peninsula, Circa 1958

Your father drives silent and one-handed, crooked left elbow riding on the window's rim. Your mother picks skin from her cuticles. You and your sister sprawl in the back seat like badly packed luggage, make faces at the skein of cars unraveling behind you. In Michigan, roads lead only to other roads: the same dotted white line, eternal border of corn and cows. You drive and drive and are never there yet.

You eat lunch at a rickety picnic table near a hill in the road where trucks grind by, farting exhaust. Your tuna sandwich tastes gassy; your Dixie cup of lemonade is hot as pee. Flies helicopter over a steaming pile of poop your parents pretend not to see. Your sister whispers you'll likely die from bad mayonnaise in an hour or so.

Hours later, your father drives silent and two-handed. Your mother picks her lip. Your sister is asleep. You are not dead. You are not there yet.

Woman's Work

Sylvia, I imagine you tidied
your kitchen before you died:
scrubbed the egg crust
from fork tines, sudsed
and rinsed your china teacup,
dried them both by hand.
You knew gas was best: no mess.
My mother never talked
about the time she went
crazy and away for a week.
She knew the courage
of shutting up, a shut
door, exquisite click
of lock. After meals,
she liked to polish
the kitchen counter
until the white Formica gleamed
her face back up at her.
Seeing herself,
she rubbed harder.

A Brief Natural History of an Eighth Grade Girl

The males [of many animal species] ... continue to vie for the prize of siring offspring via the one-celled messengers of themselves they leave as a consequence of mating: their sperm.[1]

Fuck is everywhere, scrawled in black felt pen on the stall walls of the third floor girls' room or chalked across the red brick near the bus line where the greaser boys mob like crows. You walk past them daily, a fifty-yard trudge from car to entrance, and the entire time, you feel their eyes radaring through your wool kilt down to where your white Lollipop panties hide your treasure chest. At least that's how your gym teacher makes it sound, like your tunnel down there is studded with gems so precious you need an armored car in order to make your way safely through the world. Like you should die rather than hand over the key.

... among insects and spiders, at least, ... females control much of what happens in reproduction.[2]

In the locker room after swim class, you huddle up with a dozen other girls underneath the hair dryer—a rusted udder whose nipples blow tornadoes of hot air at your scalp—and howl the lyrics to "Louie Louie" into the bristles of your hairbrush. You try not to look shocked when the girl next to you brags about almost-but-not-quite getting finger fucked by a tenth grader in his father's garage, or when she sweeps her hair up to show you two faded blue stains where he sucked her neck.

... female black field crickets in Australia let spermatophores remain attached longer for more attractive males (those singing energetic songs) than for relatively wimpy males.[3]

At night you manufacture movies in your head starring you and whatever face you paste onto a shifting cast of fantasy men—the cute lead singer for Herman's Hermits, usually, or any one of the Dave

---

[1] Marlene Zuk, "Sperm and Eggs on Six Legs," *Natural History* 119, no. 6 (June 2011): 23-35
[2] Ibid.
[3] Ibid.

Clark Five. Or the skinny ninth grader whose AV duties endow him with a spoonful of cool evident in the ease with which he threads filmstrip into projector. In your own movie, he threads your treasure chest with gold and asks you to do it, only you don't know enough about *it* to even imagine *it*, and so you fall asleep.

> ... *females of most species mate with more than one male, often in rapid succession* ...[4]

Practice makes perfect and over the years you will practice a lot. You will do it in motel rooms and basement apartments and once on the eighteenth green of a golf course on Christmas Eve. You will do it with men you call friends, with men you see once and never again, and men who are not nice. You will do it so often that you will barely recall the time before you understood what *it* entailed, only that it loomed in the distance like a city at night and how you counted down the miles until you arrived.

---

[4] Ibid.

Blissfield, Michigan: July 1969

We stared at the moon, believing we could see
Neil Armstrong bouncing around from crater
to crater, even Sue who'd called it all a crazy

hoax, a stunt taking place on the Hollywood
soundstage where they used to shoot *The Mickey
Mouse Club*. We wandered into a cornfield

and got high again and tried to find the rum
Sam had hidden that afternoon and when we
got tired, we lay on the ground and stared some

more at the sky. Billy ran his hand up my thigh
and I said *stop* though I felt lit up, all green
as in go, and when I'd run out of *no's*, I

rolled over and did it while the astronauts
and everyone watched: I did it there in the dirt.

Billy

Summer before last I parked cars at
the country club—high-class rides with seats
softer than a baby's face, as wide as beds.
Men in white dinner jackets dropped tips
in my palm, told me to watch myself
with their brand new Caddies or else.
My boss called me *kid* if we weren't busy,
hey assface when we were, threw rings of keys
at me. I used to pretend those cars were mine
and the world was my kingdom: the dimes
riding heavy in my pocket, the wives
who smelled of smoke and roses, the chime
of ice against glass, the sprinklers tossing
silvery coins of water to the grateful grass.

Donut Delite: 1969

All summer I tossed wheels of dough
into a sea of grease, where they browned
and crisped while I smoked half
a cigarette. By the time the owner
stopped by, the air would be humid
with sugar, the bakery cases filled with rows
of doughnuts I'd frosted and sprinkled.
He'd pull a buck from his wallet to pay
for his cruller, his cup of coffee, and show me
the photo of his son squinting into the light,
smiling like a man who didn't know
he would die at Khe Sanh.

On my last day the boss pressed
a wad of bills into my hand and kissed me
goodbye. When he slipped
his tongue into my mouth,
I could feel the old dog
of his heart rear up and tug
at its leash. His breath tasted
like ashes. He was my father's friend.
I was sixteen and didn't understand
yet how life can kill you a little
at a time. Still, I kissed him back.

Sex Education

How is it I recall so exactly the clatter
of film unspooling from loop
to loop, the musk of perfume radiating

from my wrists and throat, the warm gush
of Juicy Fruit, the rasp of stockings
as we crossed and uncrossed our legs. The heat

in that room, a flock of girls cooped up
away from the roosters, the almost men
of our fantasies who we dreamed

would stand beneath our windows
one day and crow for us as Romeo
had for Juliet. How we laughed

when an army of sperm ejected
from a cannon into a body
of water where they swam or died

cartoon smiles disappearing in tiny peeps
as one by one they drowned, leaving
one last lonely sperm to swim up

the long isthmus where the river
opened to an ocean, and I still recall
how the orchestra soared as he swam

and swam toward the round ship
of the egg, and how we stood
and cheered when he docked, exhausted

and triumphant, this tiny survivor,
this sturdy sperm we would spend
the next ten years trying to kill off,

and because of the stupid movie I felt
like a murderer each time I imagined him battering
frantic and headlong against the barrier

I'd erected down there, shouting
defense de la defense! as he died in spasms
of agony and once—because I was drunk

and didn't give a damn, because I wanted
only to sink into the soft chance of carelessness—
I let the whole bunch of them skinny dip

without a death sentence of chemicals
awaiting them at the end of their swim
and because I'd forgotten what

my teacher told us that day
after the film ended and the lights came up:
Remember, girls, it takes just one.

What chance did I have?
They were as fit as Olympians, cunning
as spies. They came in droves

in armies, entire Caesar's legions, coming
and coming and coming   always
so many of them and only one of me.

The Birth Mother on the Day After

My stitches pinched. The pad
bunched between my legs,
leaked blood all over
my underpants.
My jeans wouldn't zip.
All I could take away
from that place fit
into a paper bag.

In the car, my mother lit
a cigarette and said
she thought it best
if we put this mess
behind us. I said
okay. My stitches
itched. The stoplight
stuck on red.

Safe

After we buried my mother, we drank beer
and told stories in the room where she'd died.
The hospital bed was gone and the portable
commode I'd helped her settle on, the love
seat tucked flush with the window again, long
sofa shoved against the wall like always, the same
sofa where she'd fall asleep watching baseball
while she waited for me to come home from
some high school date, and once when I wasn't
home by midnight, she threw a raincoat
over her flannel pajamas and drove around
until she found me mussed and unbuttoned behind
the Big Boy, sharing a bagged can of Colt 45
with the second-string quarterback. All the way
home and for an entire week, I was punished
by silence, a vast black void of disgust. The last time
I saw her, I wanted her to speak to me, to lock
the front door and turn off the last
light, to follow me upstairs having made
the house safe for the night. But she didn't
know who I was.

The Birth Mother
on Her Daughter's First Birthday

It's late and the woman one cell over
is finally quiet. Awake, she's at war
with life, *that motherfucker*, fights
sleep when it threatens to take her down
for the night, struggling
and punching the thin sheets
to keep what she imagines is hers.
The guard says it's snowing—
a real sonofabitch to drive in—
a foot already and more to fall.
On our first date, your father
drove to the KMart parking lot
and carved figure eights in the new snow.
I sat in the passenger's seat and said
go faster because I liked
how his biceps looked
under his flannel shirt
when he yanked that steering wheel
and made that car obey him.

I should tell you
everyone's innocent
in here. Guilt is a nametag we wear
for therapy sessions, tear up
and discard on the way out.
We sit in a circle and drink
bitter coffee, tell stories
that scald the tongue.
The day you were born you felt
like a bowl of hot pasta the doctor
spilled on my stomach. The nurse said
your baby is beautiful but she was wrong.
You looked like Eisenhower,
and you were never mine,
just something I might
have borrowed for a while.

Wondrous

I'm driving home from school when the radio talk
turns to E.B. White, his birthday, and I exit
the here and now of the freeway at rush hour,

travel back into the past where my mother is reading
to my sister the part about Charlotte laying her eggs
and dying, and though this is the fifth time Charlotte

has died, my mother is crying again, and we're laughing
at her because we know nothing of loss and its sad math,
how every subtraction is exponential, how each grief

multiplies the one preceding it, how the author tried
seventeen times to record the words *She died alone*
without crying, seventeen takes and a short walk during

which he called himself ridiculous, a grown man crying
for a spider he'd spun out of the silk thread of invention—
wondrous how those words would come back and make

him cry and, yes, wondrous to hear my mother's voice
ten years after the day she died—the catch, the rasp,
the gathering up before she could say to us, *I'm okay.*

Easy

A cop caught me naked
from the waist up the night
I parked with a boy behind

a construction site, high beams
of my bare breasts white
as the bra wadded up

on the console, the dress
I sewed that afternoon
tossed over the front seat.

It looked so good I'd hated
to take it off even when he begged
me to, even as his fingers

marched up my spine, zipper's
whisk the same sound my
scissors made on first cut, crisp

and final. Hope is a dress
you assemble from three yards
of cotton, fashion a self

to step into. How easy
to give her away.

Old Flame

Decades after I quit, I still dream
of lighting a cigarette and even
in sleep feel my fingers curve to grip
the filter tip of a Newport, recall
the arc I traced, groove of hand
to lip. Do I miss smoking or the girl
who smoked, who tucked a buck
in the pocket of her cutoff jeans,
so sure the world would buy her Jack
and Coke. Or miss the men who lit
me up—flick of thumb against greased
wheel, first hit igniting tiny white lights
strung nerve to bone, clatter of engine,
rev of cells : oh axons : oh dendrites.

Depending

The rooster no longer cocks
his doodle doo at me now

that I can't hatch eggs.
Old hen: all fruitless

tubes and bristled
chin. Explaining

the sestina to freshmen
yesterday, I farted. What's

next? Leak of urine, I guess,
unexpected, like the day

in eighth grade when I felt
the pinch of a tiny hand

wring my insides: the slide,
the trickle, the long walk

to the desk for a hall pass praying
nothing showed. Years later

when I'd say *thank you*,
Jesus, or *god damn*.

Notes on "Mother Holding Child," Kodacolor Print, Circa 1952

[1] The mother is holding the child on the left side of her body, a position consistent with works by Giotto and Fra Angelico, Italian artists of the fourteenth and fifteenth centuries, both of whom painted the Christ Child on the left side of the Virgin Mary. Salk (1960, 1961, 1962, 1973) argues that by holding the infant on the left side, the mother places the infant in proximity to the beat of her heart, thereby calming the child and reassuring the mother. Indeed, the child in this photograph seems tranquil to the point of sleepiness.

[2] The mother is smiling down at the child, a pose evocative of paintings of Mary gazing at the Christ Child.

[3] The mother is dressed in a style of clothing consistent with the period, a classic shirtwaist dress informed by Dior's "New Look" of the late 1940s and early 1950. Note the hyperfeminine silhouette, how the skirt's deep pleating creates the illusion of full hips and a pinched-in waist (although it's likely the mother is wearing a girdle or long-line bra to achieve the look). Though a portion of the mother's feet have been cropped from this photograph, it appears she is wearing nylon stockings and high-heeled pumps.

[4] Paintings and other visual depictions of children supported by males or father figures are not very common and account for only four percent of paintings by artists.

[5] The mother's hair is pulled back into a ponytail, a style favored by busy young mothers during this period for its ease as well as its evocation of youth.

[6] The fading and overall yellowing of the print are typical of Kodacolor prints of this era, caused by unstable magenta dye-forming color couplers that remained in the prints after processing. Wilhelm (1993) refers to this period as "The Totally Lost Kodacolor Era of 1942–1953." The images of mother and child likely will fade and become indistinct before disappearing altogether.

[7] The mother and child stand alone in a large vacant lot, a composition that both suggests and underscores the isolation common among mid-

twentieth century women confined to their homes by young children. It was during this period that the previously agrarian landscape was largely bulldozed to make way for massive postwar suburban development.

[8] A newspaper obituary (*Daily Telegram*, April 27) lists the cause of death for the mother as cancer, one of 549,838 deaths by cancer in 1999 (American Cancer Society).

[9] City records show the lot in question had been an apple orchard.

[10] Wilhelm (1993) laments that hundreds of millions, perhaps billions, of Kodacolor prints and negatives have not survived.

Lullaby for the Daughter I Gave Away

after Beckian Fritz Goldberg's "Retro Lullaby"

Sometimes I write a letter of resignation to the universe
      and sometimes I forget to stamp the envelope, never
      without an argument. I used to believe

fact and truth were the same thing,
      though I learned to lie without smiling.

And now all I have is a picture of an old castle.

If I pin the picture above my desk,
      the prince will turn into a handsome frog,
      and he will grow a backbone and learn how
      to leap when I call him.

And I'll whisper, *it's okay, you can save me.*
      Be my sex.

I can never remember what to call him.

In fact, my father said I'd end up with a toad, a
      cold-blooded croaker. My mother used to say
      that if they drained the swamp, I'd find
      a date for the prom if I wasn't
      too picky. I moved out soon after.

Tragic, she said, to have a daughter who never writes home.

But now, at last, I've mucked
      through that swamp, arrived spry
      as a froglet at the altar of my desk
      and I forget I'm still wet and cold;
      I can't grasp a pen, and if I could

I wouldn't write home. But if I did, I'd say
      I'm okay, you can forget me. You can be
      my heavy bag.

Someday, I'll be a sore hip,
> invisible. Because the
> ink on the letter is black and forever
> and someone

will read them out loud, the Gone will haunt us

and the skeletons will barge out of closets
> and riffle through refrigerators for
> the tongues they left behind.

Let them speak. You can be my frog, my toad, my letter home.
> Be my baby. My return address.

Waitress

after Dorianne Laux

Wednesdays I waited on women golfers, endless
four tops just in from playing a hot eighteen.
They drank gallons of unsweetened iced tea,
demanded refills for free and complained
when the brew wasn't cold or strong enough. I ran
on cans of Tab, kept a lit Newport perched in a crotch
of the black ashtray in the waitress station, lucky
to get three deep drags between cocktails and order
ups. The grill cook waved a knife at me, threatened
to cut off my tits when I didn't speak up. The bartender
screamed at me for garnishing a dry Manhattan with
a maraschino cherry. I leaned on the roll warmer
and cried. No one paid attention. Every week, at least,
someone untied her black apron and said *fuck it*, walked
out in the middle of a shift never to be seen again.
I dried my eyes. In the nineteenth hole men
slipped bills in my pocket, eyed the V-neck
of my uniform whenever I set down
another round. An hour after my shift,
I was shit-faced in a bar that didn't card me,
paying for cold Molsons with quarters left
by the lady golfers. I don't remember walking home
on those nights, only the mornings when I woke to a wink
of coins on the bureau, hours before I had to punch
a clock again. I had nothing but time and I was rich.

Acknowledgments

Grateful acknowledgment is made to the editors of the following journals in which these poems, or earlier versions of them, first appeared:

Barn Owl Review: "Blissfield, Michigan: July 1969"

Brevity: "A Brief Natural History of an Eighth Grade Girl"

Burntdistrict: "Lullaby for the Daughter I Gave Away"

The Prose-Poem Project: "Postcard from the Lower Peninsula, circa 1958"

Provincetown Arts: "The Birth Mother to Her Daughter on Her First Birthday"

Rattle: "Sex Education"

The Sun: "Donut Delite: 1969," "Safe" and "Wondrous"

Grateful thanks to the National Endowment for the Arts and the Constance Saltonstall Foundation for their generous support. Thanks to mentors and teachers: Angela Estes, Kathryn Winograd and Kim Addonizio. Gratitude to writer friends for their generosity in reading and commenting on these poems—most especially Darby Knox, Jennifer Litt, Barbara Price and Melanie Graham. Special thanks goes to Veronica Kornberg for her wisdom, kindness and encouragement.